JUV/
QP
251.5
.P368
2004
ORIOLE

DEC 2005

Chicago Public Library

W9-ANU-152

Reproduction

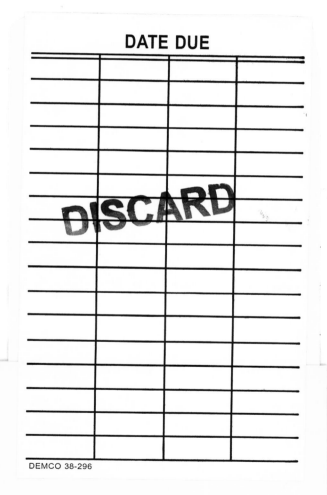

DATE DUE

DISCARD

DEMCO 38-296

Oriole Park Branch
7454 W. Balmoral Ave.
Chicago, IL 60656

OUR BODIES

REPRODUCTION

Steve Parker

Raintree

Chicago, Illinois

Titles in the series:
The Brain and Nervous System • Digestion
The Heart, Lungs, and Blood • Reproduction
The Senses • The Skeleton and Muscles

© 2004 Raintree
Published by Raintree, a divison of Reed Elsevier, Inc.
Chicago, Illinois
Customer Service 888-363-4266
Visit our website at www.raintreelibrary.com

All rights reserved. No part of this book may be reproduced or transmitted in any form or by any means, electronic, or mechanical, including photocopying, recording, taping, or any information storage and retrieval system, without permission in writing from the publisher. Every effort has been made to contact copyright holders of any material used in this book. Any omissions will be rectified in subsequent printings if notice is given to the publisher.

For information address the publisher:
Raintree, 100 N. LaSalle, Suite 1200, Chicago, IL 60602

Library of Congress Cataloging-in-Publication Data:

Parker, Steve.
  Reproduction / Steve Parker.
      v. cm. -- (Our bodies)
Includes bibliographical references and index.
Contents: Introduction -- Female parts -- The female cycle -- The first week -- Child to adult.
  ISBN 0-7398-6623-0 (lib. bdg.-hardcover)
  1. Human reproduction--Juvenile literature. [1. Reproduction.] I. Title. II. Series.
  QP251.5.P368 2004
  612.6--dc21

                          2003010547

08 07 06 05 04
10 9 8 7 6 5 4 3 2 1
Printed and bound in China

Picture Acknowledgments:

p. 1 Topham Picturepoint (Image Works); p. 4 Corbis (Walter Hodges); p. 5 Still Pictures (J. Alcalay and B Marcon); pp. 7, 28, 32, 40, 43(top) Alamy; p. 9 Science Photo Library (Dr. Yorgos Nikas); p. 11 Science Photo Library (John Burbidge); p. 13 Digital Vision; p. 15 (top) Science Photo Library (CNRI); p. 17 Science Photo Library (Prof. P. Motta/Department of Anatomy, Univ. La Sapienza, Rome); p. 16 Science Photo Library (D. Philips); p. 19 Science Photo Library (Andy Walker, Midland Fertility Services); p. 21 Science Photo Library (Hank Morgan); p. 23 Science Photo Library (Alexander Tsiaras); p. 25 Ardea (John Cancalosi); p. 27 Corbis (Laura Doss); p 29 Science Photo Library (Astrid & Hanns-Frieder Michler); p. 31 (left) Science Photo Library (SIU School of Medicine); p. 31 (right) Science Photo Library (Stephen J. Krasemann); p. 33 Science Photo Library (BSIP Astier); p. 35 Science Photo Library (top) (John Cole); p. 35 (bottom) FLPA (Eddie Schuiling); p. 36 Corbis (Ariel Skelley); p. 37 Topham Picturepoint (Image Works); p. 39 Science Photo Library (Saturn Stills); p. 41 Science Photo Library (Andy Levin); p. 44 Corbis (Tom Stewart); p. 45 Nature Picture Library (Peter Oxford).

Front cover (inset) Science Photo Library (CNRI).

CONTENTS

R0405744441

Oriole Park Branch
7454 W. Balmoral Ave.
Chicago, IL 60656

INTRODUCTION

A vital process

Reproduction is a vital feature of life. It means that living things make or produce more of their own kind—they "have babies." All forms of life reproduce, from the tiniest germs and worms to gigantic whales and redwood trees. Each living thing has special parts that work together to reproduce, or breed. These parts are known as the reproductive system.

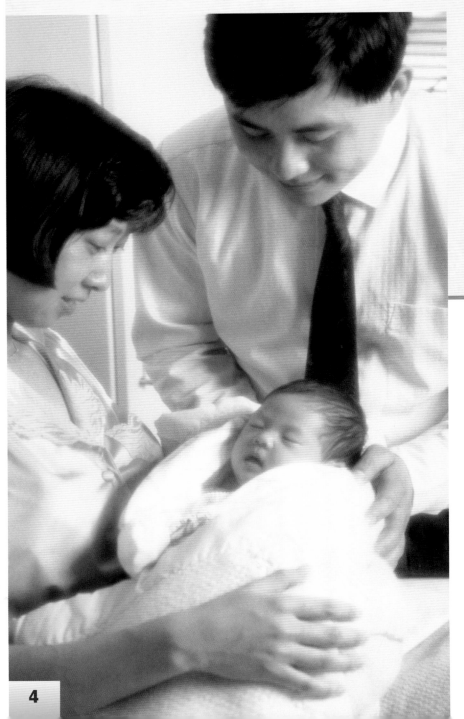

The start of a new life. These parents now have a new family member who will drastically change their daily routine.

Stages of reproduction

The main parts of the reproductive system, and the way they work, are similar in a huge range of animals and also in humans. The process of reproduction happens in several stages. A female and male get together and mate, or have sexual intercourse. Inside the female's body, a tiny **sperm cell** from the male joins or fertilizes a tiny **egg cell** from the female to make a fertilized egg. The fertilized egg cell, which is smaller than the dot on this letter *i*, multiplies and starts to form a baby, which grows over weeks and months inside the mother's body. This is the time of **pregnancy.** After the baby is born, it continues to grow bigger and stronger over weeks, months, and years. Gradually it becomes a mature adult who is able to reproduce.

Views about reproduction

The ways that people describe human reproduction and their views about sex, pregnancy, birth, and growing up vary hugely around the world. These views and attitudes are often based on culture and tradition. They can differ from one nation to another, among various faiths and ethnic groups, among people of different ages and backgrounds, and even among different members of a family.

A baby orangutan receives devoted care and attention from its mother for three years or more. The mammals called primates (monkeys, apes, and humans) are known for long periods of parental care.

FEMALE REPRODUCTIVE ORGANS

Female system

There are many sizes, shapes, and ages of human bodies, from small to large, thin to wide, and young to old. But each is either one sex or the other—female or male—depending on its reproductive parts. The main parts of the female reproductive system, also called the sex organs, are the **ovaries,** oviducts (fallopian tubes), **uterus** (womb), **cervix,** and vagina.

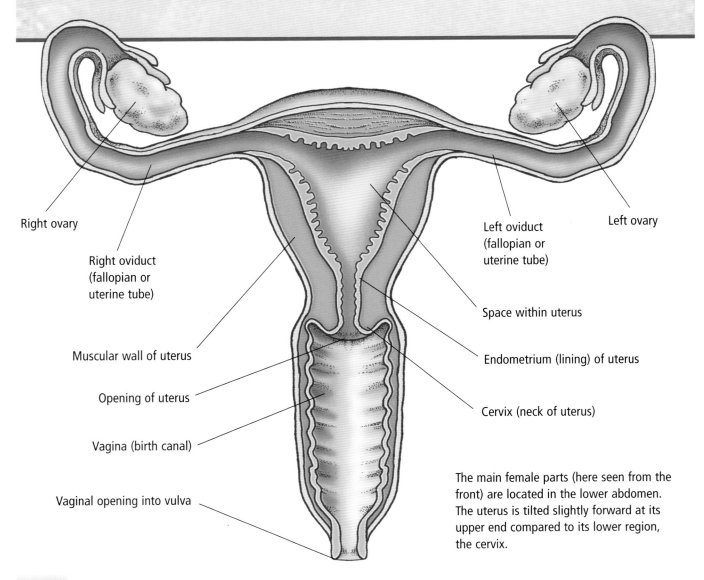

Right ovary

Right oviduct (fallopian or uterine tube)

Muscular wall of uterus

Opening of uterus

Vagina (birth canal)

Vaginal opening into vulva

Left oviduct (fallopian or uterine tube)

Left ovary

Space within uterus

Endometrium (lining) of uterus

Cervix (neck of uterus)

The main female parts (here seen from the front) are located in the lower abdomen. The uterus is tilted slightly forward at its upper end compared to its lower region, the cervix.

Ovaries

Each of the two ovaries is a slightly flattened egg shape, a little smaller than a thumb, and located in the side of the lower **abdomen,** just below the level of the navel ("belly button"). About once every four weeks, one of the ovaries releases a tiny **egg cell** for the reproductive process, as shown on page 10.

Oviducts and uterus

The released egg cell passes into the oviduct, also called the fallopian tube, egg tube, or uterine tube. This is about 4 inches (10 centimeters) long and carries the egg toward the uterus. The uterus is about the size and shape of an upside-down pear, tilted forward in the base of the abdomen. If the egg cell is joined by a **sperm cell,** it starts to grow and develop into a baby inside the uterus.

Cervix and birth canal

The rearmost, lower, narrow "neck" of the uterus is called the cervix. Its opening leads into the vagina, or birth canal, which is about 3 to 3.5 inches (8–9 centimeters) long and opens to the outside of the body at the lower front, between the legs. When a baby is born it passes out of the uterus, through the cervical opening, and along the vagina to the outside. The outer part of the vagina is called the vulva.

ANIMAL VERSUS HUMAN

A human baby develops inside its mother for nine months. This time is called **pregnancy,** or gestation. Animals that are similar in size to humans have similar gestation times. In small creatures such as mice, the gestation time is much shorter, two to three weeks. In the largest land animal, the elephant, it is 22 months. A baby elephant weighs about 220 pounds (100 kilograms)—30 times heavier than a human baby!

THE MENSTRUAL CYCLE

A four-week process

For an **egg cell** to join with a **sperm cell,** it must be released from its **ovary.** This is called **ovulation,** and it usually takes place about once every four weeks. It also usually happens in alternate ovaries—first the left, then the right ovary, then the left, and so on. The four-week process of egg ripening and release, and preparation of the **uterus** for the baby, is called the **menstrual cycle.**

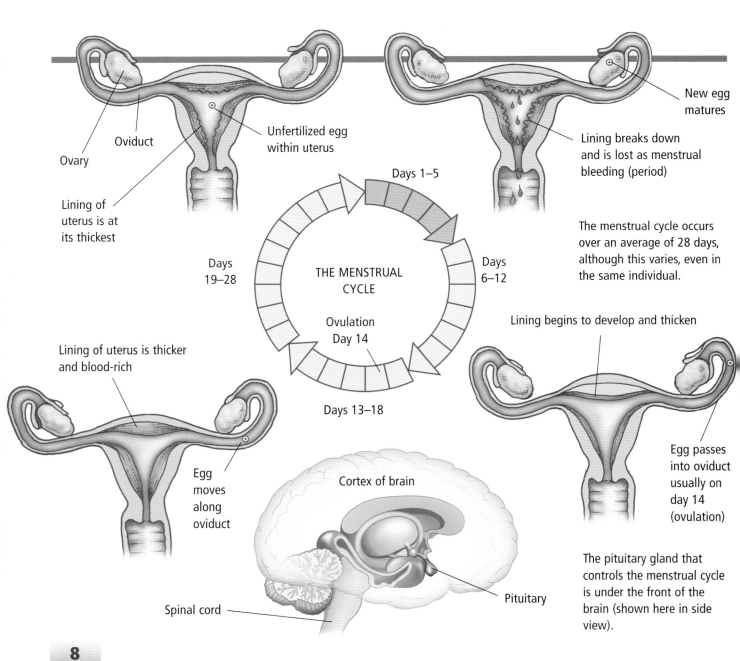

Ovary

Oviduct

Unfertilized egg within uterus

Lining of uterus is at its thickest

New egg matures

Lining breaks down and is lost as menstrual bleeding (period)

Days 1–5

Days 19–28

THE MENSTRUAL CYCLE

Days 6–12

Ovulation Day 14

Days 13–18

The menstrual cycle occurs over an average of 28 days, although this varies, even in the same individual.

Lining begins to develop and thicken

Lining of uterus is thicker and blood-rich

Egg moves along oviduct

Cortex of brain

Pituitary

Spinal cord

Egg passes into oviduct usually on day 14 (ovulation)

The pituitary gland that controls the menstrual cycle is under the front of the brain (shown here in side view).

Hormones

The cycle is controlled by four natural body chemicals, or **hormones:** estrogen, follicle stimulating hormone (FSH), luteinizing hormone (LH), and progesterone. Estrogen is the main female hormone, made in the ovaries. At the start of the cycle, estrogen makes one of the egg cells begin to ripen inside a tiny fluid-filled container, or **follicle,** within the ovary (see next page). Estrogen also makes the inner lining of the uterus thicken with blood-rich tissues, preparing it to receive the fertilized egg. The next hormone, FSH, is made in the **pituitary gland,** just under the front of the **brain.** It travels in the blood to the ovary and causes the follicle to grow larger and the egg to ripen further.

Ovulation

Next, LH, also from the pituitary gland, causes the egg to be released, or ovulated, and ready for **fertilization.** This usually happens halfway through the cycle. Then, the empty follicle still in the ovary makes a fourth hormone, progesterone. This keeps the inner lining of the uterus thick and blood-rich, ready to nourish the egg cell if it has joined with a sperm cell. If the egg and sperm do not join, the thickened lining of the uterus is not needed, so it breaks down. With the egg it is lost through the **cervix** and vagina, as the menstrual blood flow, or period. Each period lasts

MICRO BODY

The uterine lining is called the endometrium. In the first phase of the menstrual cycle it becomes much thicker and filled with extra blood vessels, under the control of estrogen. In the second phase it stays thickened and blood-rich, under the control of progesterone.

Microscopic cells of many kinds multiply in the uterus lining, at about day ten of the cycle.

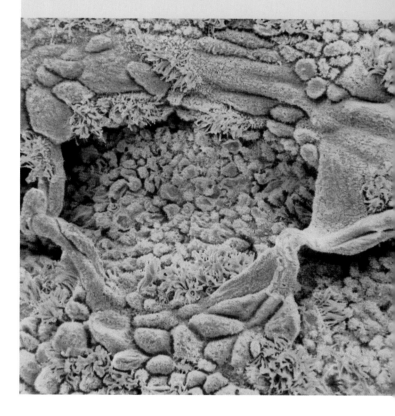

an average of four to seven days and, on average, 2 ounces (60 milliliters) of blood are lost in total each month. The first day of the period is counted as day one of the next menstrual cycle, and the whole process begins again. Periods usually start between the ages of 11 and 16 and stop between ages 45 and 55.

EGG PRODUCTION

The eggs ripen

At the beginning of each menstrual cycle, about fifteen to twenty **egg cells** begin to ripen in one of the **ovaries.** Each egg is in a tiny baglike container, the **follicle,** and each follicle enlarges as it fills with fluid. The batch of follicles is just under the outer covering of the ovary, known as the germinal **epithelium.** As the follicles fill with fluid and enlarge, they move deeper into the underlying part of the ovary, which is called the medulla.

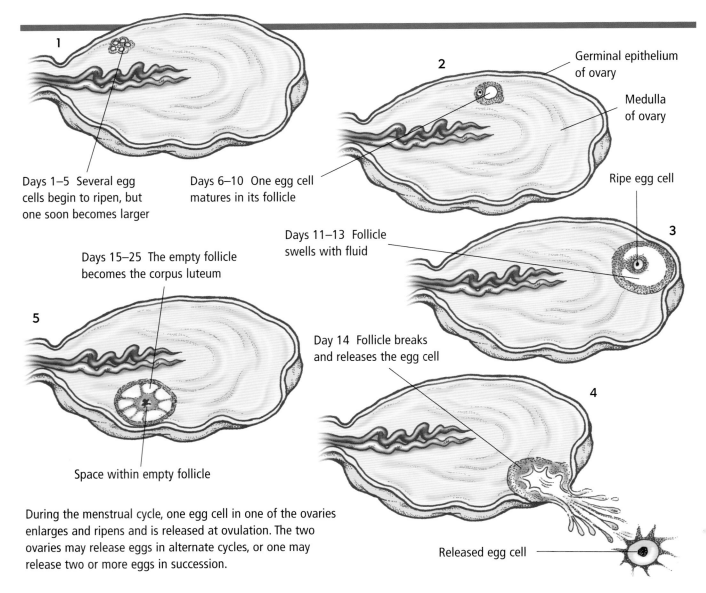

Days 1–5 Several egg cells begin to ripen, but one soon becomes larger

Days 6–10 One egg cell matures in its follicle

Germinal epithelium of ovary

Medulla of ovary

Ripe egg cell

Days 11–13 Follicle swells with fluid

Days 15–25 The empty follicle becomes the corpus luteum

Day 14 Follicle breaks and releases the egg cell

Space within empty follicle

Released egg cell

During the menstrual cycle, one egg cell in one of the ovaries enlarges and ripens and is released at ovulation. The two ovaries may release eggs in alternate cycles, or one may release two or more eggs in succession.

Ovulation

Usually only one egg cell from the batch that begins to develop reaches the final stage of ripening each month. Its follicle enlarges to several millimeters across and moves outward from the medulla of the ovary to form a small bulge at the ovary's surface. Under the influence of luteinizing **hormone,** the follicle breaks, or ruptures, and releases its fluid and the egg cell, which is now about one-tenth of one millimeter across. This stage is called **ovulation.** The released egg cell then passes into the funnel-shaped opening of the oviduct, which is very close to the ovary. If the egg joins a **sperm cell,** this usually happens in the oviduct (see page 17).

After ovulation

The egg cell leaves behind an empty follicle in the ovary. This becomes thickened and filled with a yellowish material that makes hormones, especially estrogen and progesterone. It is about .4 inches (10 millimeters) across and known as the corpus luteum, or "yellow body."

MICRO BODY

The fully ripe egg cell sits within fluid in its bubble-like follicle. The egg cell is surrounded by a mass of other microscopic cells. These other cells look tiny compared to the egg, but, in fact, they are the normal size for body cells—the egg itself is relatively huge.

The fluid-filled ripe follicle (large pink area) with the egg cell in its lower left part dominates the ovary.

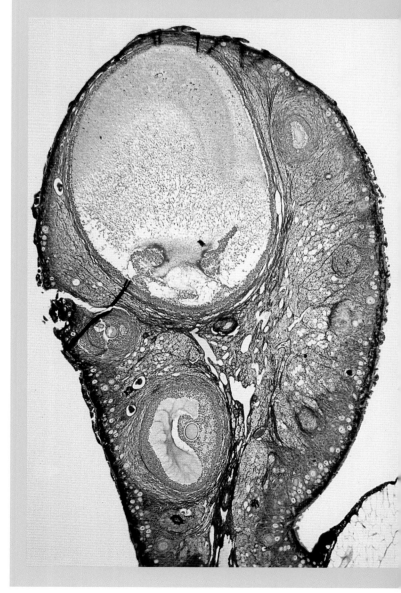

MALE REPRODUCTIVE ORGANS

Male system

The main parts of the male reproductive system, also called the sex organs, are the **testes,** epididyms, sperm ducts (vas deferens or ductus deferens), seminal glands (seminal vesicles), prostate gland, and penis. Unlike the female reproductive parts, which are within the lower **abdomen,** most of the male parts are below the abdomen, with the testes contained in a baglike pouch of skin called the scrotum.

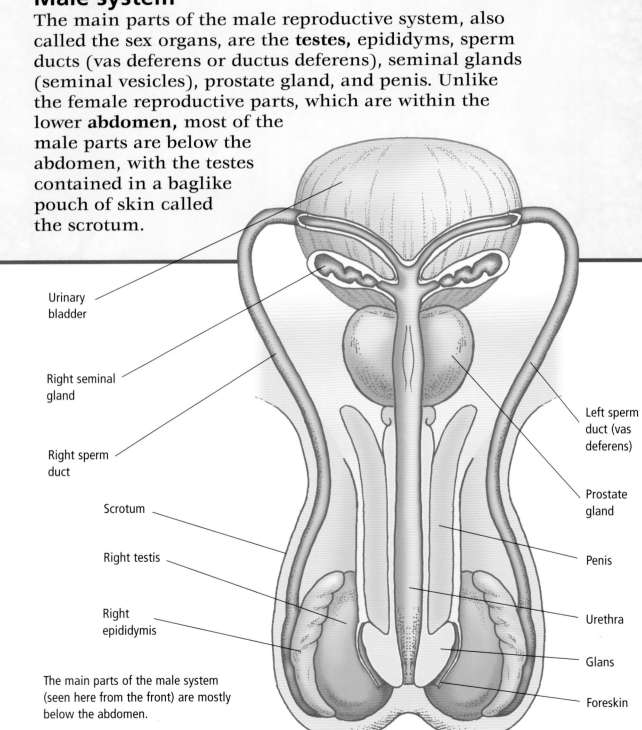

Urinary bladder

Right seminal gland

Right sperm duct

Scrotum

Right testis

Right epididymis

Left sperm duct (vas deferens)

Prostate gland

Penis

Urethra

Glans

Foreskin

The main parts of the male system (seen here from the front) are mostly below the abdomen.

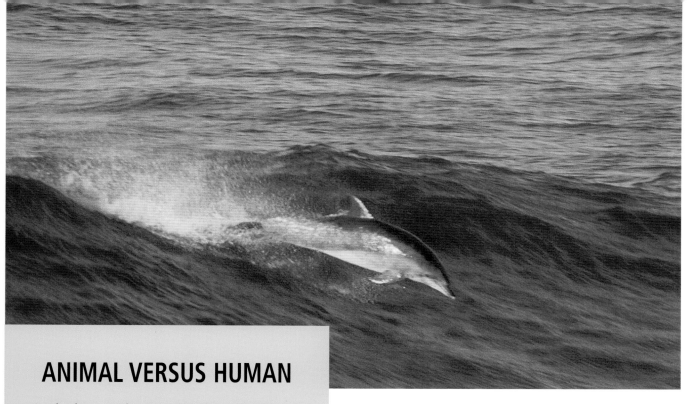

ANIMAL VERSUS HUMAN

In the human the sperm-making testes are outside the main lower body, or abdomen. In many animals the testes are contained within the abdomen. In a male dolphin, the penis is also partly contained within the abdomen, covered by a flap of skin. This creates a smooth, streamlined body shape when swimming.

The testes

Each of the two rounded testes (testicles) is 1.5 to 2 in. (4 to 5 cm) across. Inside, millions of sperm are produced every day (see page 14). They pass into the epididymis, which is a very thin tube about 20 ft (6 m) long, joined to the upper and outer side of the testis and coiled tightly around it. From each epididymis another thin tube, the sperm duct, carries sperm toward the penis.

Tubes and glands

Each sperm duct goes from its epididymis up into the lower abdomen, where it meets and joins a tube from the thumb-sized seminal gland. This happens on each side of the body. The left and right tubes join and lead through the middle of the prostate gland where yet another tube joins them—the **urethra.** This comes from the bladder just above the prostate gland. The seminal and prostate glands add nourishment-containing fluid to the **sperm cells** before they leave the body along the urethra. This runs along the middle of the penis and opens at its end or tip. At different times the urethra carries different substances: sperm cells in their semen or seminal fluid during sex (see page 16), or urine from the bladder during urination.

SPERM PRODUCTION

Millions of cells

The male reproductive system produces millions of **sperm cells** every day. The process begins in the **testes** or testicles, which are made of many small, tightly coiled tubes called seminiferous tubules. There are 600–800 in each testicle, and their lengths added together would be about 220 yards (200 meters).

Epididymis

Sperm-carrying ducts from testis to epididymis

Coils of seminiferous tubules

Main sperm duct (vas deferens)

Septum divides lobes of testis

Tunica (tough covering of testis)

This front view of the right testis is cut away to show the hundreds of coiled tubes, called seminiferous tubules, where sperm are made and become mature.

Inside the testis

The seminiferous tubules are lined inside by microscopic round cells called spermatogonia. These are specialized to divide rapidly and produce **cells** known as spermatocytes. Gradually these are pushed toward the middle of the tube, as the spermatogonia around the edge continue to divide. Each spermatocyte changes shape from a round blob to a tadpole-like shape with a rounded head and a long, thin, flexible tail. This is a sperm cell, or spermatozoon. Each sperm cell takes about two months to develop.

MICRO BODY

Each of the seminiferous tubules in the testis is about 20 inches (50 centimeters) long but only one-fifth of a millimeter wide. Inside, spermatogonia cells around the edge multiply to make spermatocytes, which gradually change shape to form tadpole-like sperm cells near the center.

This enlarged image shows sperm cells in stages of development (blue), those in the center with long tails, within the narrow seminiferous tubule (pale orange).

Epididymis

As sperm cells form, they pass along the fluid in the middle of the seminiferous tubules, which join to the single tube of the epididymis, coiled around the testis. Here, the sperm cells become mature and are stored for up to a month. If they do not leave the body through the penis, they slowly break down into tiny pieces. The whole process of sperm production is controlled by the **hormone** testosterone, made in the testes. In turn, the production of testosterone is controlled by two hormones, **follicle** stimulating hormone and luteinizing hormone, made by the tiny **pituitary gland** at the base of the **brain** (see page 8).

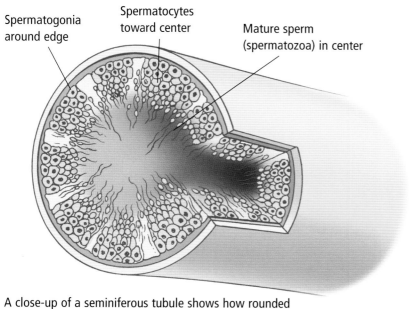

Spermatogonia around edge

Spermatocytes toward center

Mature sperm (spermatozoa) in center

A close-up of a seminiferous tubule shows how rounded spermatogonia develop into mature sperm cells (right).

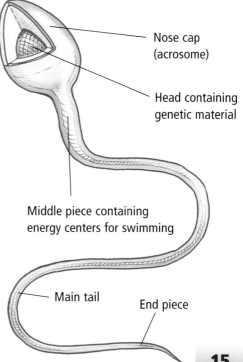

Nose cap (acrosome)

Head containing genetic material

Middle piece containing energy centers for swimming

Main tail

End piece

THE REPRODUCTIVE PROCESS

Crucial timing

A human **embryo** begins when a ripe **egg cell** joins a mature **sperm cell** to form a fertilized egg. There are various events that must take place so that this can happen, and their timing is very important.

MICRO BODY

The egg cell is smaller than the dot on this *i*, but it is still many times larger than the sperm cells. Many sperm swarm around the egg, but when one sperm has joined with it, a barrier hardens around the egg to prevent other sperm from reaching it.

Hundreds of sperm cells (cream color) swarm around the huge egg cell (blue) and try to join or fuse head-first with it. Only one will succeed.

Journey of the sperm

Sperm leave the male body through a process called ejaculation. This involves the tightening, or contraction, of muscles around the epididymis, prostate gland, and seminiferous tubules, which pushes sperm cells from the two **testes** and epididymes along the sperm ducts and into the **urethra**.

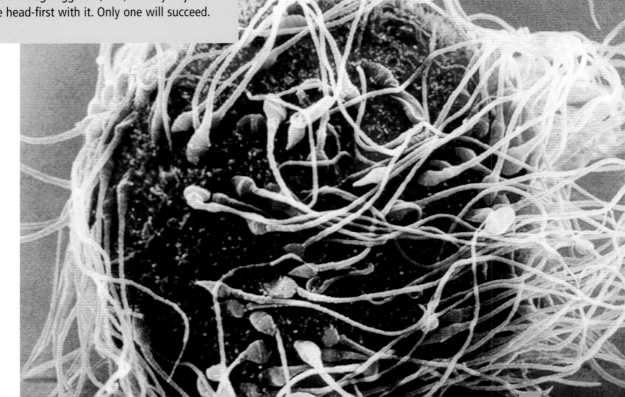

There are about 300 to 500 million sperm cells in nourishment-packed fluids from the seminal and prostate glands. The tadpole-shaped sperm lash their long, thin tails and swim on their journey out of the tip of the penis. During sexual intercourse, when the penis is in the vagina of the female body, the sperm are released into its upper part. From here the sperm swim through the **cervix** into the **uterus.** Throughout the journey, millions of sperm cells die.

Journey of the egg

Usually an egg cell is ready and able to join with a sperm cell for only one to two days after **ovulation.** Unlike sperm cells, the egg cell cannot actively swim. It moves very slowly along the oviduct, wafted along by tiny hairs called **cilia** in the lining of the tube. Meanwhile, the sperm swim from the uterus into the two oviducts. Of the millions that begin the journey, perhaps several thousands will reach the ripe egg cell in one of the oviducts. Just one of these sperm cells joins with the egg, at **fertilization.**

Twins

If one egg is fertilized and then divides, and each of these two cells develops into an embryo, the result is two babies with the same genetic material: identical twins. If two eggs

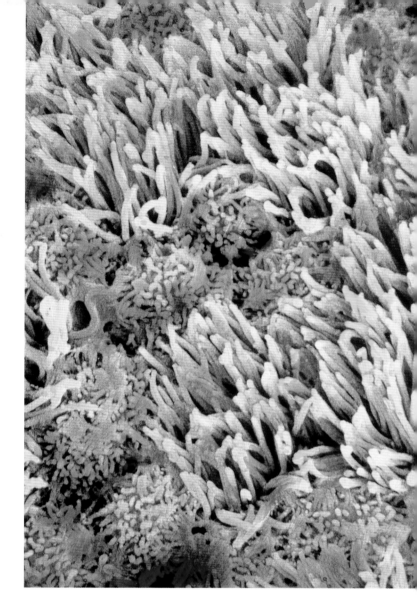

The lining of the oviduct (egg duct), between the **ovary** and uterus, has millions of waving micro-hairs called cilia (yellow). Scattered between them are secretory cells (purple) that make fluids and mucus to smooth the egg's passage.

are released together and each is fertilized by a sperm, the result is nonidentical, or fraternal, twins. These children are as similar to each other as any sisters or brothers born to the same parents.

THE FIRST WEEK

Instructions for development

The **egg cell** and **sperm cell** each contain tiny threads known as chromosomes, which carry chemicals of the substance DNA, arranged into groups called **genes.** These contain the instructions for how the baby will grow and develop—for instance, whether it will be male or female, have light or dark skin, or have brown or blue eyes. Most **cells** in the human body have 23 pairs of chromosomes. The egg and sperm each have only 23, one of each pair. When an egg and sperm join together, they complete the 23 pairs of chromosomes to make the full set of genes for the new baby.

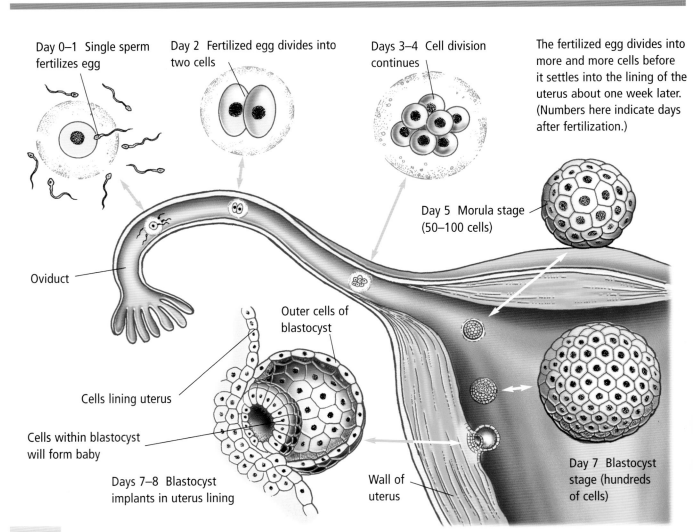

Day 0–1 Single sperm fertilizes egg

Day 2 Fertilized egg divides into two cells

Days 3–4 Cell division continues

The fertilized egg divides into more and more cells before it settles into the lining of the uterus about one week later. (Numbers here indicate days after fertilization.)

Day 5 Morula stage (50–100 cells)

Oviduct

Outer cells of blastocyst

Cells lining uterus

Cells within blastocyst will form baby

Days 7–8 Blastocyst implants in uterus lining

Wall of uterus

Day 7 Blastocyst stage (hundreds of cells)

From oviduct to uterus

After one or two days, the fertilized egg cell divides in half, into two cells. About twelve hours later, these two cells also divide, forming four cells. Then, the same division happens to give eight cells, sixteen, and so on. This gradually forms a tiny, blackberry-like ball of cells, still passing slowly along the oviduct. After about five to seven days there are 100-plus cells in the ball shape with a hollow, fluid-filled center. This is the blastocyst. The original egg cell was so much bigger than other types of cell that only now, after many divisions, the cells of the blastocyst reach normal body cell size.

Implantation

Seven or eight days after **fertilization,** the blastocyst settles into the thickened lining of the **uterus,** where it receives nourishment for further growth and development. This stage is known as implantation. The cells continue to divide, and now they also start to grow, using nutrients from the uterus lining around them. The blastocyst begins to develop rapidly into an embryo. The whole process of fertilization, implantation, and the start of **pregnancy** is called conception.

The main pale, shadowy object in the center of this micro-photograph is a six-day blastocyst, with the individual cells just visible as fuzzy outlines. (The other cells to the top left are from the original egg's outer covering.)

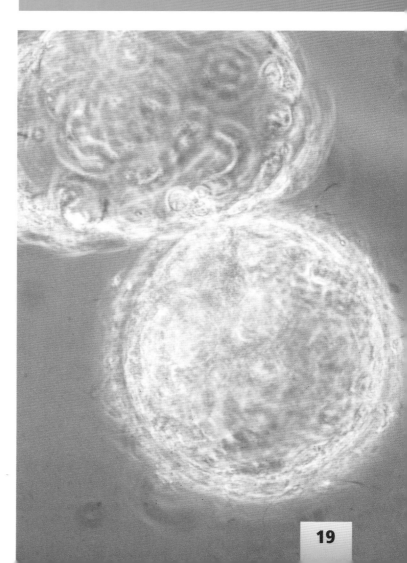

Top Tips

The healthy development of the **fetus** depends greatly on the mother's health. Harmful chemicals such as drugs, tobacco smoke, or alcohol can interfere with the fetus's development during pregnancy. Pregnant women therefore should not take drugs or medication (unless advised to by a doctor), drink alcohol, smoke, or spend time in smoky rooms. A woman who may become pregnant should also take care to eat a healthy diet and perhaps take supplements such as folic acid, as advised by a doctor, to help ensure that the baby is healthy.

REPRODUCTIVE PROBLEMS

A number of reasons

There are many reasons why sex does not always lead to **pregnancy** when a woman wants to become pregnant. They include problems when sex takes place or with the reproductive systems of the man or woman. Most reproductive problems are found in people over the age of 30.

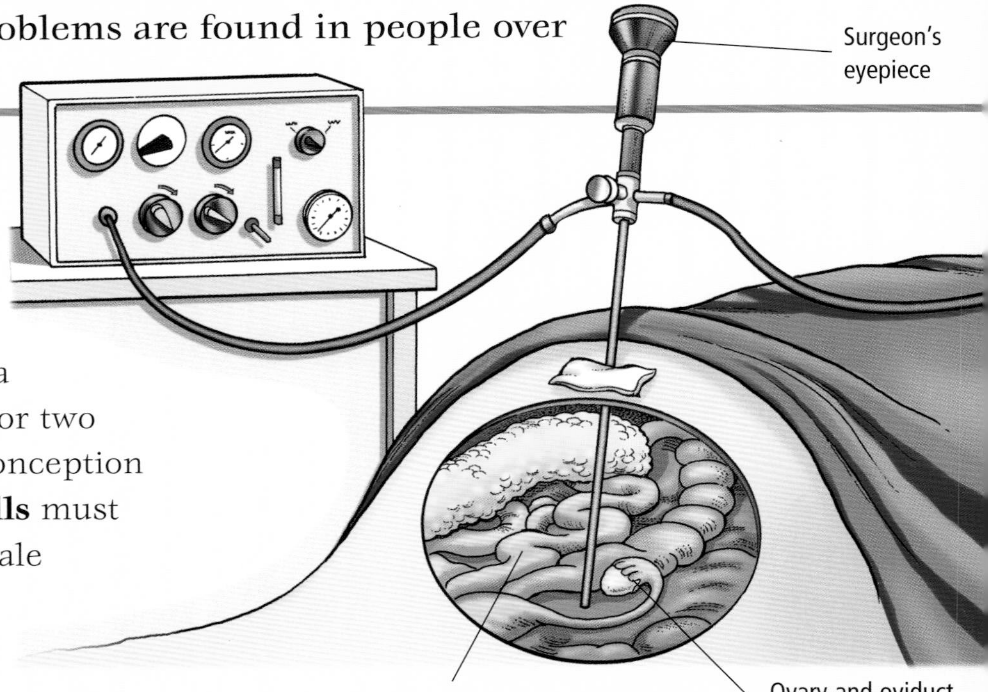

Surgeon's eyepiece

Timing

The **egg cell** is alive and healthy and able to join with a sperm only for a day or two after ovulation. For conception to happen, **sperm cells** must be present in the female reproductive parts at this time. Also, the sperm themselves can survive in the female reproductive parts for only three to four days. So, usually, sex must happen within a day or two before or after **ovulation** for the egg to be fertilized (see pages 16–17).

Intestines and other abdominal organs

Ovary and oviduct within abdomen

This cutaway diagram shows how the laparoscope is inserted through a small incision to see inside the abdomen.

In the male

Only one sperm is needed to fertilize the egg, but millions are required to ensure that this happens. If the man produces fewer than 20–30 million sperm each time, the chances of conception can be greatly reduced. This "low sperm count" has many causes, from a previous illness or injury to stress or tiredness, or from taking various drugs, including alcohol and some perscription drugs. Sometimes medication to increase sperm production can help.

In the female

In some women hormonal control of the menstrual cycle does not work properly, and so an egg does not ripen or is not ovulated, or the lining of the womb is not prepared. Previous illness or infection in the lower **abdomen**, known as the pelvic region, can also damage reproductive parts. A general term for this is PID, pelvic inflammatory disease. There are many treatments for such problems, ranging from perscription drugs and **hormones** to various operations. Another option is to collect eggs and sperm so that they can be joined outside the body and then, once the eggs are fertilized, be placed in the woman's **uterus.** This is known as in vitro fertilization.

Top Tips

The male's main reproductive parts are outside the abdomen and are easily damaged. During risky activities, including many sports, boys and men are advised to wear protective equipment such as an athletic support or jockstrap. An injury may affect sperm production and the ability to become a father.

A medical worker watches a microscope image on a monitor screen of an egg cell being held on the end of a glass tube called a pipette (visible on the left of the screen). The needle (to the right) will inject the genetic material from a sperm directly into the egg.

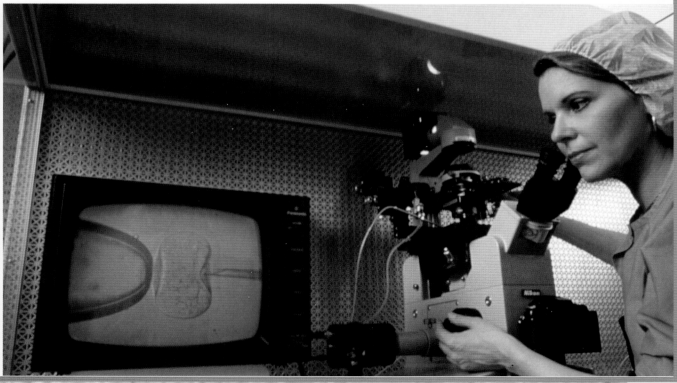

THE EARLY EMBRYO

Dividing cells

About ten days after **fertilization,** the tiny ball of **cells** known as the **embryo** has settled into the thickened lining of the **uterus.** Its cells continue to divide and grow and start to form a small disc inside the ball. This will become the baby itself, while the layers around it will become the bag-like containers or membranes within the uterus (see page 26).

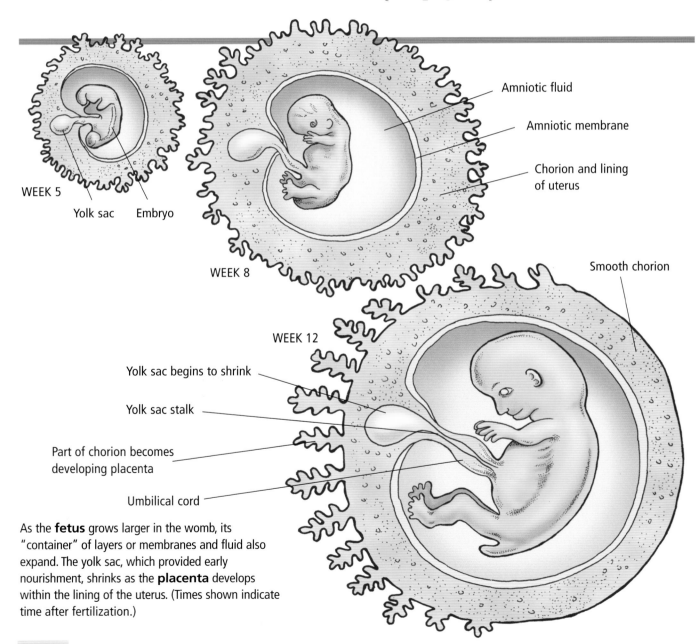

Amniotic fluid

Amniotic membrane

Chorion and lining of uterus

WEEK 5

Yolk sac   Embryo

WEEK 8

Smooth chorion

WEEK 12

Yolk sac begins to shrink

Yolk sac stalk

Part of chorion becomes developing placenta

Umbilical cord

As the **fetus** grows larger in the womb, its "container" of layers or membranes and fluid also expand. The yolk sac, which provided early nourishment, shrinks as the **placenta** develops within the lining of the uterus. (Times shown indicate time after fertilization.)

This view into the womb shows the yolk sac at about four weeks after fertilization. Blood vessels over its surface carry its nourishment to the embryo (which is not in this view).

MICRO BODY

During very early development, the tiny embryo gains nourishment from a baglike part called the yolk sac. This contains nutrient-rich yellow yolk, similar to the yolk in a hen's egg. Starting at six weeks after fertilization, the yolk sac shrinks away, and the embryo is nourished through the placenta (see pages 26–27).

taking shape, and tiny bumps called limb buds appear on the body. These will grow into arms and legs. The whole embryo would fit into this O.

The body takes shape

Two weeks after fertilization the tiny disc of the embryo is less than one millimeter across. Its cells continue to divide and grow into hundreds and then thousands. They also begin to move around and build the shape of the new baby. About three weeks after fertilization, the embryo is the size and shape of this c. Yet inside its tiny body, parts such as the heart and **brain** are forming. After four weeks, the head is

The second month

During the second month, development of the baby continues very rapidly. The head is large compared to the body as the brain, eyes, ears, and mouth form. Major body parts such as the lungs, stomach, intestines, and muscles are also taking shape. About eight weeks after fertilization, the whole embryo is hardly larger than a grape. Yet all its major body parts have formed, even its eyelids, fingers, and toes.

GROWTH IN THE UTERUS

The changing fetus

After two months in the **uterus,** the developing baby is no longer known as an **embryo,** but as a **fetus.** It has all its major body parts and organs, and its heart has begun to beat. During the next seven months the main changes will be an increase in size and the formation of smaller body features such as eyelashes, fingernails, and toenails.

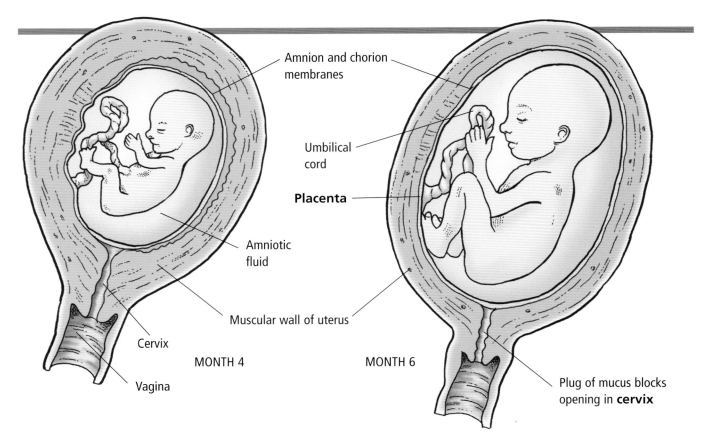

Amnion and chorion membranes

Umbilical cord

Placenta

Amniotic fluid

Muscular wall of uterus

Cervix

MONTH 4

Vagina

MONTH 6

Plug of mucus blocks opening in **cervix**

The middle third

During the middle third of **pregnancy,** months four to six, the fetus continues to grow rapidly, from 1.2 in. (30 mm) in length to almost 12 in. (300 mm). During the fourth month, its reproductive parts become visible on the outside of its body, so it is possible to see, using a scan or

As the baby enlarges, it has less room to move inside the uterus. (Times shown indicate time after **fertilization.**) The mother usually notices her **abdomen** beginning to bulge in the third or fourth month.

similar method of imaging, if the baby is a girl or boy. Blood is flowing through the blood vessels, and a covering of thin, fine hair begins to grow on the body.

Months five and six

During the fifth month the muscles and **skeleton** become stronger. The fetus begins to move—simple stretching at first, then enacting more controlled movements such as kicking the legs and clenching the fingers. The heart pumps blood at the rate of about 150 beats per minute. During the sixth month, the fetus grows rapidly longer and looks slim. Its movements become more complicated and even include thumb-sucking. The skin is covered by a slippery, creamy layer of a substance called vernix. Small body details continue to form, such as the eyebrows.

By the ninth and last month in the uterus, the baby is very cramped. It has usually turned upside down, ready to be born head-first.

ANIMAL VERSUS HUMAN

Compared to a new human baby, a new baby marsupial like an opossum is tiny and at an early stage of development. Born after only about seventeen days inside its mother, it is smaller than a grape, with no fur, closed eyes and ears, and paddle-like legs. It crawls to the mother's pouch, where it spends five more months continuing to develop. Once in the pouch it nurses from its mother's teat.

LIFE SUPPORT IN THE UTERUS

Protective layers

Inside the **uterus** it is dark and quiet. The developing baby is surrounded by a liquid called amniotic fluid, and two thin, baglike layers of membranes, the amnion and chorion. In the early stages when the **fetus** is very small, it can float in its fluid and membranes. But after about six to seven months, the baby becomes cramped and cannot stretch easily. Although the uterus continues to enlarge around it, the baby has much less room for movement.

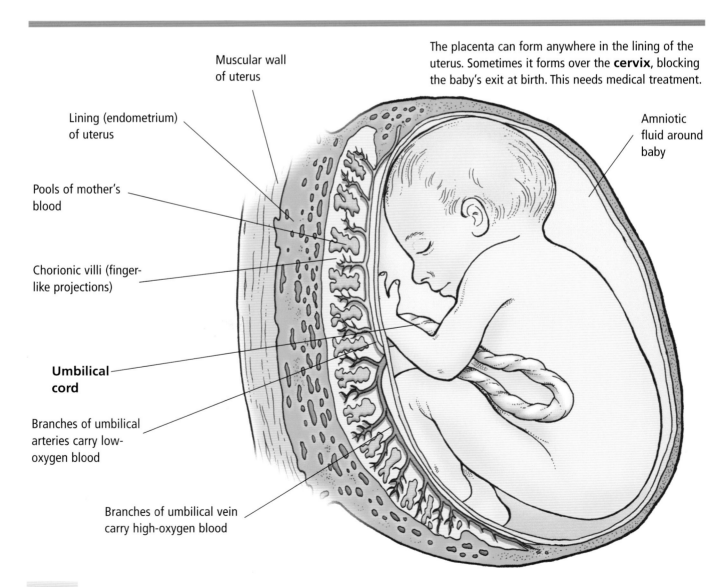

Muscular wall of uterus

Lining (endometrium) of uterus

Pools of mother's blood

Chorionic villi (finger-like projections)

Umbilical cord

Branches of umbilical arteries carry low-oxygen blood

Branches of umbilical vein carry high-oxygen blood

The placenta can form anywhere in the lining of the uterus. Sometimes it forms over the **cervix**, blocking the baby's exit at birth. This needs medical treatment.

Amniotic fluid around baby

Vital needs

In the uterus, the baby cannot feed itself or breathe air. Nutrients and **oxygen** come from the mother's body, through a part called the **placenta.** This is shaped like a plate and develops in part of the thickened lining of the uterus. The baby's blood flows to the placenta along two vessels (tubes), the umbilical **arteries,** within a rope-like part, the umbilical cord. Blood in these arteries takes oxygen and nutrients from the mother's blood in the placenta and passes waste substances from the baby in the opposite direction. The baby's blood then flows along another vessel in the cord, the umbilical **vein,** back to the baby's body.

Changes in the mother

The first sign that a woman is pregnant is usually when her next period (menstrual bleeding) does not occur. Hormonal changes keep the lining of the womb thickened to nourish the tiny **embryo.** By the fourth month of **pregnancy** the mother can feel and see her enlarged uterus, and by five months, she can detect the baby moving. She also gains weight due to the baby itself and also the fluids, membranes, placenta, enlarged uterus, and other parts.

Toward the end of pregnancy, the baby and uterus push the mother's abdominal organs up against her chest, and the extra weight at the front affects her posture.

MICRO BODY

Inside the placenta, the baby's blood flows through tiny tubes surrounded by the mother's blood. The two sets of blood do not mix, but nutrients and oxygen can easily pass through the thin layer separating them.

Growing in size

During the last couple of months of **pregnancy,** the mother's **abdomen** enlarges greatly as the baby and **uterus** get bigger. They press upward on her chest, so she may become short of breath, particularly when lying down or when walking or exercising. The mother's breasts enlarge as they prepare to produce milk to feed the newborn baby. By the eighth month of pregnancy, the typical baby is about 18 in. (450 mm) long and weighs 5.5 lbs (2.5 kg). However, the combination of the mother's enlarged uterus, with its fluids and membranes, and other bodily changes means she gains about 20–30 lbs (9–13 kg).

Many women choose to have ultrasound scans done during pregnancy.

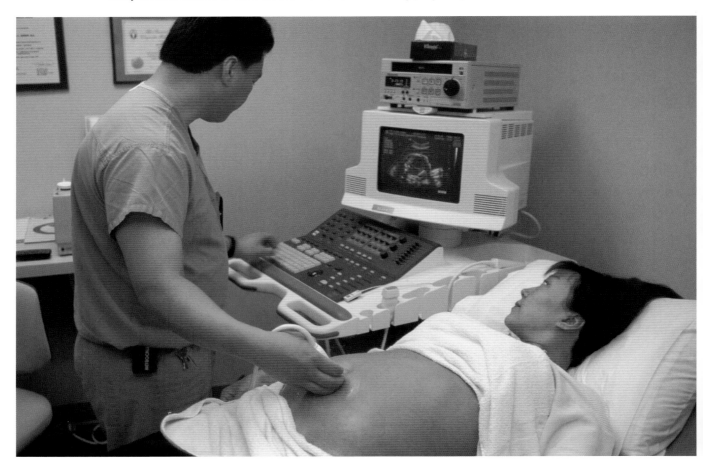

MICRO BODY

During pregnancy the mother's breasts enlarge as the **mammary glands** grow bigger within them. The glands are packed with large **cells** that make and release milk. The milk then passes along tubes called lactiferous ducts to the nipple, the darker, raised part of the breast. When the newborn baby sucks the nipple, milk will be released.

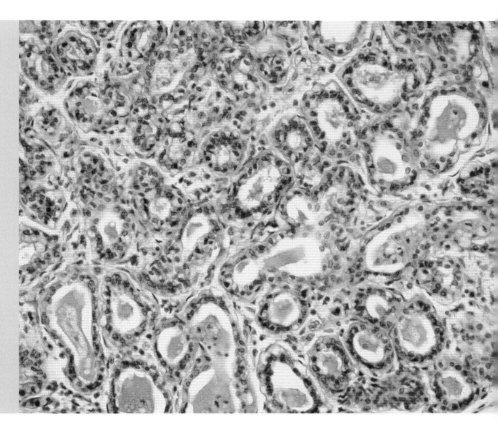

Milk-making cells are arranged in curved layers (dark pink/purple), each enclosing a central space (very pale pink). Many of the central spaces here contain drops of milk and other products (medium pink).

Seeing the fetus

Starting at about eight weeks, pregnant women should get regular prenatal ("before birth") checkups. Sometimes a type of body scan called an ultrasound is carried out to ensure the **fetus** is developing normally. The scanner beams ultrasound waves (too high-pitched for us to hear) into the mother's abdomen. These waves bounce off the fetus and other parts inside, and a computer analyzes the reflections, or echoes, to form a picture of the fetus in the uterus. The mother may also be offered other tests to ensure the health of her and her baby.

The last month

By the last month of pregnancy, the hair on the baby's head has usually started to grow, and the baby looks increasingly "chubby" because of a thickening layer of fat under its skin. Around this time the baby usually turns upside down, ready to emerge from the uterus head-first. This is a safe way to be born, since the rounded head gradually stretches open the **cervix** and birth canal, and then the body, arms, and legs follow without getting stuck or crossed over.

THE DAY OF BIRTH

The role of hormones

Pregnancy is closely controlled by **hormones** in the mother's body. The main hormone is hCG, human chorionic gonadotrophin. It is made in the **placenta** and helps the **uterus** and placenta develop properly. The typical "pregnancy test" sometimes used to confirm conception detects hCG in the mother's blood or urine.

Labor

As the day of birth approaches at about nine months, another hormone takes over. This is oxytocin, released into the mother's blood by the **pituitary gland** at the base of her **brain.** Oxytocin causes the powerful muscles in the stretched walls of the uterus to shorten, or contract. This presses the baby against the **cervix** (uterine opening). At first the contractions occur every 20–30 minutes. Gradually they become more powerful and frequent, coming every 3–5 minutes. This time is called the first stage of labor, or simply "labor." When the bag-like membranes around the baby tear and allow the fluid in the uterus to flow out of the vagina, people say that the woman's "water breaks."

Birth

The baby's head presses harder on the cervix, which opens wider. Eventually the baby's head can begin to pass out of the uterus and into the birth canal. Strong contractions continue and push the baby along the birth canal so that it can emerge into the outside.

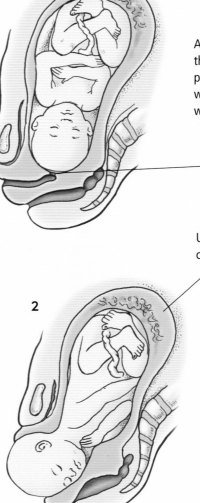

1

As labor progresses, the baby's head presses on the cervix, which is becoming wider or dilated.

Cervix

Uterine muscles contract

2

Eventually the cervix is wide enough for the baby's head to pass through into the birth canal.

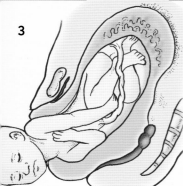

3

The baby's shoulders follow as delivery proceeds and the baby is born.

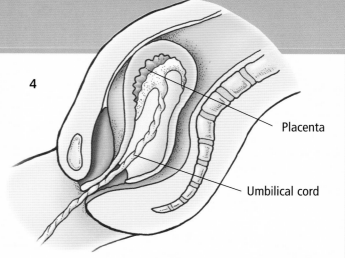

4

Placenta

Umbilical cord

The placenta comes away and is also expelled from the uterus.

This is known as the second stage of labor, or delivery. Soon after, the placenta comes away from the inner lining of the uterus and also emerges. This is the third stage, or afterbirth. Once the baby is safely born, the umbilical cord linking it to the placenta can be clamped or cut.

After a strenuous and tiring birth, the new baby meets its mother face to face.

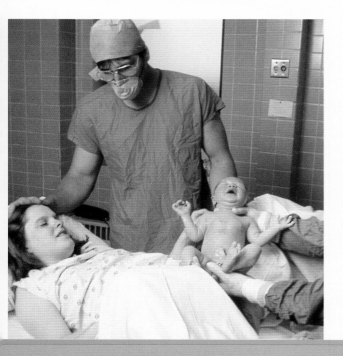

ANIMAL VERSUS HUMAN

The time taken for a human birth varies hugely. On average, it is 14–15 hours for a mother's first baby, and less for additional pregnancies. In many animals, it happens much faster. An antelope or gazelle gives birth in 15–30 minutes, and after another 30 minutes, the youngster is able to run. This speedy birth means the mother and baby antelope are at risk for the shortest possible time from predators such as lions.

A NEW BABY

The first breath

Birth is extremely tiring for both mother and baby. As the baby emerges, it sees lights, hears loud noises, and feels fresh air, all for the first time. The sudden changes may cause it to cry loudly. Crying opens the baby's air passages and lungs, helping the baby to breathe for itself. This is helpful, given that the baby's supply of **oxygen** from the **placenta** will soon cease, because the placenta has broken away from the **uterus** and the **umbilical cord** has been clamped or cut.

It often takes a few attempts for both the mother and the baby to get used to breastfeeding. Usually it becomes a natural routine.

Feeding

After birth, the baby no longer receives nourishment through the placenta, so it must use its digestive system. The most natural way for the baby to feed is to suck milk from the **mammary glands** in its mother's breasts. The production of milk is controlled by a **hormone** called prolactin, while the release of milk from the breasts as the baby sucks is controlled by oxytocin. Both these hormones come from the mother's **pituitary gland.**

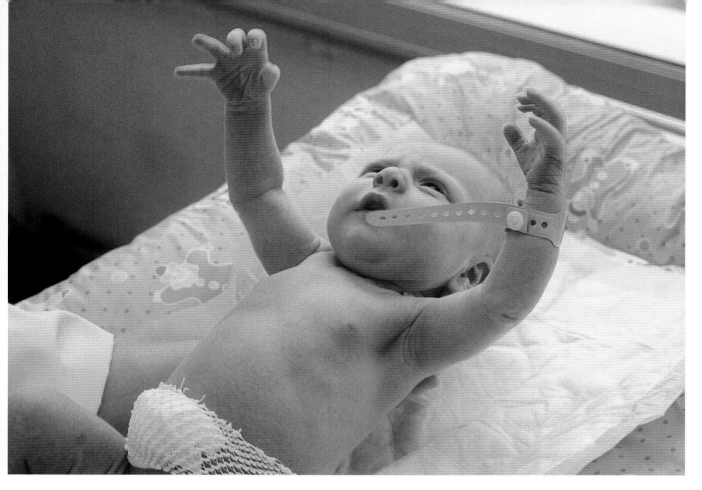

Daily routine

The new baby sleeps for 18 to 20 hours out of every 24. It usually wakes up and will perhaps cry when it is hungry, hot, cold, or uncomfortable—for example, in need of cleaning and diaper changing. The new baby cannot control its bladder or bowels, and so it empties these when they are full through an automatic body reaction called a **reflex.** The baby has other reflexes, too. If startled by a sudden movement or loud noise, it throws its arms out and cries. It will also grip an object placed in its hand. These reflexes and other body processes are tested as part of the postnatal ("after birth") checkup by medical staff to ensure the baby is healthy.

When a new baby is lowered briefly and quickly as part of its checkup, it shows a startle reflex by throwing out its arms and legs, trying to grab with its hands, and crying out. This reflex continues until about two to three months of age.

Try this!

If you know a new baby, ask the baby's parents if you can touch its cheek very gently with your finger. The baby turns its head toward your finger, its lips ready to suck. This automatic reaction is the rooting, or sucking, reflex, and it helps the baby to find the mother's nipple and feed on milk.

BIRTH PROBLEMS

Physical changes

Birth is a stressful and complicated time, with many changes in both the baby and mother. It is also a very physical event. The pregnant mother's **uterus** is the largest and most powerful muscle in her body, and as it contracts strongly, the baby is squeezed with considerable force through the birth canal. The skull bones inside the baby's head are not yet joined together or fully hardened. As the baby leaves the uterus, the bones can bend and move slightly while still protecting the **brain** inside. This allows the head, which is the baby's widest part, to change shape so it can slide more easily through the **cervix** and birth canal.

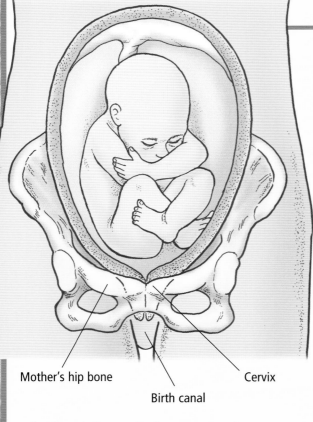

Mother's hip bone

Birth canal

Cervix

In a breech (bottom-first) presentation the baby may be facing the front, as shown here, sideways, or facing its mother's back.

Problem presentations

Most babies are born head first (see page 31), and this is known as cephalic presentation. However, in some cases the bottom part of the baby's body tries to emerge first, which is called breech presentation. Coming out of the uterus in these positions is much more awkward, and the baby may get stuck. Doctors may be able to twist the baby into the correct position or use spoonlike devices called forceps to ease it out. In some cases an operation may be necessary. In a cesarean section, doctors make careful incisions or cuts through the walls of the mother's **abdomen** and uterus, remove the baby, and then sew up the incisions. This operation may also be used to remove a baby that has become ill before birth.

Premature babies

A baby born before the usual time of nine months is said to be premature. The earlier it is born, the smaller and weaker it usually is, and the more in need of special care. It may be kept warm in a boxlike container called an incubator and provided with extra **oxygen** to help its breathing. However, babies born less than one month premature are not usually in great danger.

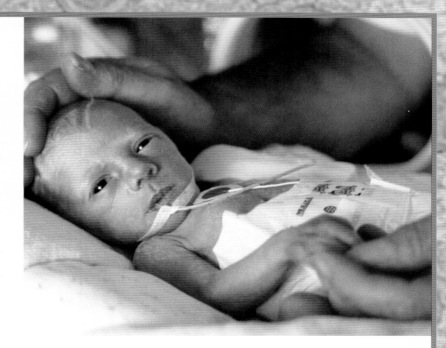

A premature baby may be fitted with sensors to monitor its heartbeat, and perhaps a mouth tube for fluids.

The tenrec is a shrew-like animal from Madagascar. It may have more than 20 babies in one litter, but many soon die.

ANIMAL VERSUS HUMAN

In humans, about one birth in 85 is two babies, called twins (see page 17). About one birth in 7,500 is three babies, or triplets, and one in 500,000 is four babies, or quadruplets. Some animal mothers usually have many more babies at one time—in rare cases, more than 30!

GROWING UP

Infancy

The period of infancy lasts from about one month after birth until the young child can walk, which is, on average, at one year of age. The body grows faster during infancy than at any other time after birth. Most healthy babies weigh three times more at one year old than they did at birth. In particular, the baby's **brain** almost doubles in weight, from about one-quarter to one-half of its eventual adult size.

Motor skills

Learning new knowledge, skills, and abilities does not begin at school. It happens from birth and is incredibly rapid during infancy. Part of this learning involves movements and actions. After three months, a typical baby can reach out and grasp a toy or other object and roll over when lying down. By six months it sits up unaided and puts food, or anything else it is holding, into its mouth. By nine months it may crawl on its hands and knees and begin to stand up while holding a support. These physical abilities are known as **motor** skills. They depend on the quick development of many body parts, including muscles, nerves, and especially the brain, which controls and coordinates the movements.

Eating may seem easy now, but at the age of one or two, it is a very tricky process and is very messy to learn!

Mental abilities

An infant also develops many new **mental,** or mind-based, skills. As early as six weeks of age, it learns that if it smiles at a human face, it will get a response when people smile and talk back. The infant improves its abilities to look and listen and learns to recognize familiar faces and voices. By a year old, a typical infant can say a few simple words, such as names of family members or pets.

Babies rapidly learn to identify their close family members by sights, sounds, and smells. They also learn that if they smile, they will get a reaction and more attention.

Try this!

An infant's change of diet, from milk to other foods, or "solids," is called weaning. It happens at widely differing ages, often not just for the nutritional needs of the baby itself, but for reasons of the parents' tradition, culture, or lifestyle. In general, young children prefer fairly sweet foods. Ask family members and friends of different ages which foods they like, such as ice cream, chocolate, onions, or spicy dishes such as chili. Is there a gradual change with age, from preferring sweet foods to stronger-flavored spicy or seasoned ones?

THE YOUNG CHILD

Slowing down and speeding up

Between the ages of one and five years, the body's rate of growth gradually slows. But learning physical and **mental** skills gets ever faster. Inside the **brain,** thousands of new connections form every day between its various parts. These represent memories such as words and names, the appearances of people and places, and the ability to carry out actions and movements. By fifteen to eighteen months a typical young child can use a spoon at mealtimes, kick and throw a ball, and control the bladder **reflex** while awake so that urination happens only at certain times. By four years old the child is able to get dressed and undressed, hop and skip, and talk in full sentences.

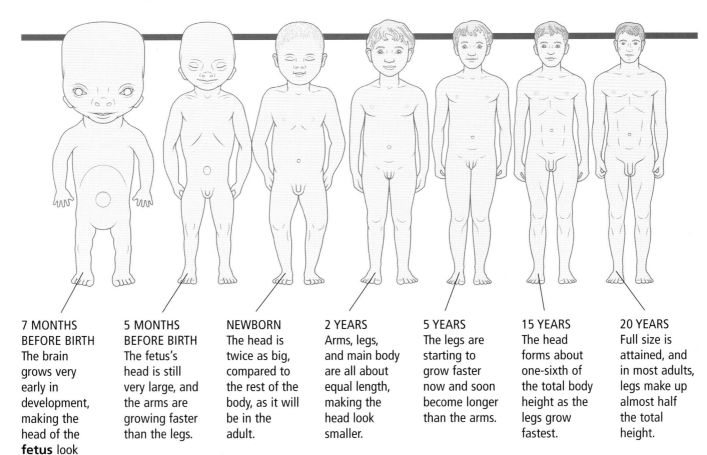

7 MONTHS BEFORE BIRTH
The brain grows very early in development, making the head of the **fetus** look huge.

5 MONTHS BEFORE BIRTH
The fetus's head is still very large, and the arms are growing faster than the legs.

NEWBORN
The head is twice as big, compared to the rest of the body, as it will be in the adult.

2 YEARS
Arms, legs, and main body are all about equal length, making the head look smaller.

5 YEARS
The legs are starting to grow faster now and soon become longer than the arms.

15 YEARS
The head forms about one-sixth of the total body height as the legs grow fastest.

20 YEARS
Full size is attained, and in most adults, legs make up almost half the total height.

In these diagrams of growth at different stages, before and after birth, all the bodies are drawn to be the same height. This shows how the proportions change, especially the size of the head compared to the body and legs.

Try this!

How tall were you on your second birthday? You might have been measured then at a regular medical checkup. Or you might be able to figure out your height from a birthday photograph. In most people, body height at two years old is about half the height of the body when it is fully grown. However, growth is affected by many events—for example, it may slow during an illness.

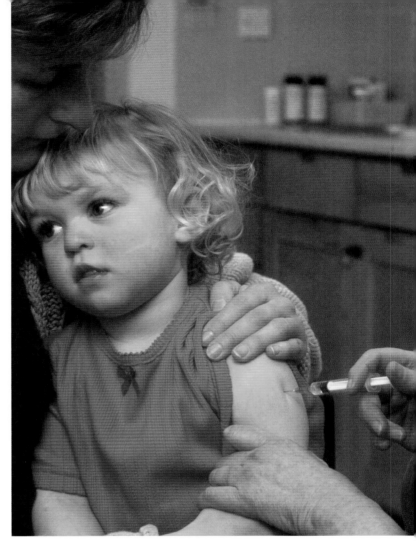

Immunization may bring a moment's tearfulness, but for most children (except in special circumstances) it also gives years of protection against infectious diseases that can be disabling or even deadly.

Protection against disease

Many kinds of harmful microbes, or germs, can invade the body and cause illness. For some of these, once the body has suffered the illness and recovered, the next time it encounters the germs, it can kill them very quickly before they cause disease. This ability to recognize and fight disease is called resistance, or immunity. In vaccination or immunization, harmless versions of the germs (or the chemicals they produce) are put into the body, usually by injection. The body does not suffer from the illness, but it does develop immunity against it.

Childhood immunizations

In the United States most babies and children receive a carefully planned series of immunizations to protect them against possibly dangerous diseases in future. The times of the injections and the diseases vary, but they may include polio, diphtheria, tetanus, pertussis (whooping cough), measles, mumps, rubella (German measles), and perhaps tuberculosis (TB).

Developing skills

Throughout childhood, to the age of about ten to twelve years, the body's growth rate gradually slows down. However, its **mental,** or mind-based, progress increases at great speed. A young child learns in many different ways. He or she develops language skills such as understanding new words and putting them together in a meaningful way as sentences. Further physical abilities and **motor** skills rely on the increasing coordination of body muscles, such as learning how to draw, write, ride a bicycle, or play a musical instrument.

Team sports encourage children to stay healthy and also to work with others and cooperate as part of a group.

Behavioral changes

There are also huge developments in behavior (what the child thinks, says, and does, and how she or he gets along with family and friends). Younger children tend to think mainly of themselves, want whatever they see immediately, and ignore the wishes of others. Gradually they learn how to share, interact with others, and make friends. This type of learning does not take place only in daycares and schools. It takes place at home, when playing, out shopping, in the car, taking part in sports, just about everywhere. All of these advances contribute to the growth and development of the child's whole body.

Medical checkups

Development during childhood can be measured at arranged checkups with health workers and medical staff. But a child's growth can also be monitored in a less official way by parents and family members. If there is cause for concern, for example, if a child is slow to learn to talk or read, expert advice should be obtained sooner rather than later. Usually there is no great problem and the child soon catches up as part of the normal variation among different people. But if there is a significant problem, then early help is likely to be more successful.

MICRO BODY

Apart from the **brain,** the body parts that change most during childhood are the bones of the **skeleton.** In a young child, the bones are partly made of cartilage, a substance that is slightly softer and more flexible. Cartilage is less likely to break during the knocks and falls that children often suffer. Gradually, by eighteen to twenty years of age, the cartilage parts of the bones harden into true bone.

A regular check on growth, especially measuring height and weight, takes just a few minutes. It gives reassurance that all is well or detects any problem early, so that it can be dealt with sooner.

Puberty

When a baby is born, the only parts of its body that are not working are the reproductive parts. These begin to develop fully after childhood, and the body's growth also speeds up greatly at this time, which is called **puberty.** The age of puberty varies greatly. It may start anywhere between nine and sixteen years of age. The process usually occurs a year or two earlier in girls than boys. It also takes a shorter time in girls, two to three years, compared with three to four in a boy.

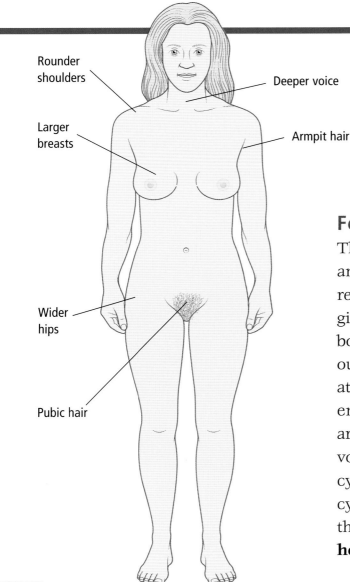

Rounder shoulders

Deeper voice

Larger breasts

Armpit hair

Wider hips

Pubic hair

Most girls go through the same physical changes during puberty, in the same sequence. However, there is huge variation in the times at which these occur, and some changes are less marked in certain women than in others.

Female changes

Throughout childhood, the overall size and shape of the body (apart from the reproductive parts) is much the same in girls and boys. During puberty, the female body grows rapidly in height, then its outline becomes more rounded, especially at the shoulders and hips. The breasts enlarge, hair grows under the arms and around the vulva and vagina, and the voice deepens slightly. The menstrual cycle gradually begins, with the first full cycle known as the menarche. Most of these changes are controlled by the **hormone** estrogen, from the **ovaries.**

Adolescence is the phase of life that includes puberty, and for most people, it corresponds to the teenage years. It is a time of increasing independence.

Top Tips

As the body matures, it becomes important to check the health of the reproductive parts. Women are advised to have this done at yearly exams by a gynecologist. A gynecologist is a doctor who specializes in women's reproductive health. Men are advised to examine their testes on a regular basis. Pain, lumps, or other changes should be reported promptly to a doctor. Usually the cause is not serious, but whatever the problem, early treatment has a greater chance of being successful.

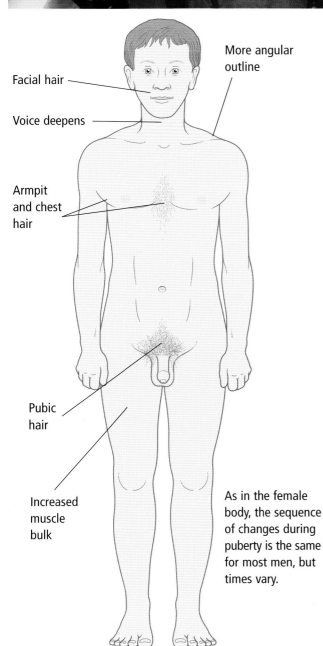

Facial hair

Voice deepens

Armpit and chest hair

Pubic hair

Increased muscle bulk

More angular outline

As in the female body, the sequence of changes during puberty is the same for most men, but times vary.

Male changes

On average, the male body grows faster than the female during puberty, so that it ends up slightly taller. The male body's outline also becomes more angular, with a greater proportion of muscle. Hair grows on the face, under the arms, and around the penis and scrotum. The voice "breaks," or "cracks," and then becomes much deeper because the voicebox in the throat grows rapidly at this time. The **testes,** penis, and other reproductive parts enlarge and sperm production begins. Most of these changes are controlled by the hormone testosterone, from the testes.

THE NEXT GENERATION

The ability to reproduce

The human body reaches adulthood and grows to its tallest height and greatest all-around physical ability at the age of 20 to 25 years. Its ability to reproduce usually begins before this, at **puberty** (see pages 42–43), and lasts for many years. In most women at about the age of 50 the menstrual cycle gradually becomes less regular and then ceases. This time is known as menopause. In men sperm production begins to reduce slowly from the age of 30, but it may continue to 70 years old or more.

Aging

In general, after 40 years old the body shows signs of aging. Muscles become less powerful, bones slightly weaker, joints slightly stiffer, the heart and

Many people stay fit and active well into their later years. At any age, a positive attitude helps enjoyment of life.

ANIMAL VERSUS HUMAN

In more developed countries, most people live to 75 to 80 years of age, and some to more than 100. Yet certain animals live far longer. In general, bigger animals live longer. But the rare lizard-like tuatara of New Zealand does not begin to breed until it is 25 years old, may still be reproducing when it reaches 100, and lives to perhaps 140!

lungs less efficient, the skin more wrinkled, the reactions slower, and the senses such as sight and hearing less sharp. But the aging process is so variable that in some people it is not noticed until 60 years old or later. **Mental** abilities such as learning may also become slightly slower. However, experience shows that people who stay active mentally all through their lives tend to have less mental deterioration as they become older.

Medical checkups

Regular medical checkups are important all through life, but their details change with age, from baby to young adult to older person, according to the risks of ill health at each stage.

The reproductive cycle

The body's reproductive parts are not essential for the life of the body itself. Indeed, to treat certain diseases, one or more reproductive parts may be surgically removed. However, reproduction is essential for humankind to survive. We have a reproductive cycle, just like other forms of life—babies are born, grow into youngsters, and become mature adults who can have babies of their own.

GLOSSARY

abdomen lower part of the main body or torso, below the chest, it contains mainly the parts for digestion, excretion, and reproduction

artery blood vessel with thick, muscular walls that carries blood under high pressure away from the heart

brain incredibly complex part of the body in the upper part of the head, it is made of billions of nerve cells and nerve fibers. The brain receives information from the senses, controls the body's movements, and is the site of thoughts, memories, conscious awareness, and the mind.

cell single unit, or "building block," of life. The human body is made of billions of cells of many different kinds.

cervix main opening, or "neck," of the uterus

cilia microscopic hairlike parts that can waft or wave back and forth, such as those lining the nasal chambers inside the nose

egg cells small, single cells made in the female reproductive parts, one of which joins with a sperm to begin development of a baby

embryo name for a developing human body during its earliest stages from fertilization through eight weeks

epithelium layer covering the surface of a body part or forming its inner lining

fertilization joining of an egg cell and sperm cell to form the fertilized egg, which begins to develop into a new human body

fetus name for a developing human body from eight weeks after fertilization until birth

follicle in the female reproductive system, a baglike structure containing fluid and an egg cell, which enlarges as the egg cell becomes mature, or ripe, and ready to be released

genes instructions in the form of the chemical DNA for how the body grows, develops, and maintains itself

hormones natural body chemicals made by parts called endocrine glands, that circulate in blood and control many processes such as growth, the use of energy, water balance, and the formation of urine

mammary glands parts of the female body, within each breast, that make milk to feed a newborn baby

menstrual cycle approximately four-week cycle that happens in mature females. During the menstrual cycle an egg ripens and is released for possible fertilization. The uterus is also prepared for the implantation of an embryo.

mental based in the brain or mind, and concerned with thinking and behavior

motor in the body, having to do with movements or motions, such as motor nerves that carry signals to the muscles to control their movements

ovaries two female reproductive parts that produce egg cells and also make hormones that control female development and the reproductive cycle

ovulation release of the mature, or ripe, egg cell from its baglike container, the follicle, in the ovary

oxygen gas making up one-fifth of air, it has no color, taste, or smell, but it is vital for breaking down nutrients inside the body to obtain energy for life processes

pituitary gland tiny part under the front of the brain inside the head that makes many different hormones and controls various bodily processes such as growth and development

placenta plate-shaped reproductive part that develops in the lining of the uterus after implantation of the embryo. It passes oxygen and nutrients from the mother's blood system to the blood system of the developing baby

pregnancy time when a baby is growing and developing inside its mother's uterus, before birth

puberty time when the body grows rapidly and the reproductive parts begin to function

reflex quick, automatic reaction by the body to a sudden change or situation that could be harmful, such as blinking the eyes if something comes near them

skeleton all of the body's bones and also the supporting parts made of cartilage

sperm cells tiny single cells made in the male reproductive parts, one of which joins with an egg to begin development of a baby

testes (only one is called a testis) two male reproductive parts that produce sperm cells and also make hormones that control male reproductive development

umbilical cord cord coming from the navel that connects a fetus to the placenta. This is how the developing fetus gets nourishment.

urethra tube leading from the urinary bladder to the outside, along which the waste liquid, urine, passes during urination

uterus female reproductive part in which the baby grows and develops before birth, also known as the womb

vein blood vessel with thin walls that carries blood under low pressure back to the heart

FURTHER INFORMATION

BOOKS

Gold, Susan Dudley. *The Endocrine and Reproductive Systems.* Berkeley Heights, N.J.: Enslow, 2003.

Kranz, Rachel. *Reproductive Rights and Technology.* New York: Facts on File, 2002.

Lamb, Kristen. *Pregnancy.* Chicago: Raintree, 2001.

Parker, Steve. *The Reproductive System.* Chicago: Heinemann, 2003.

Royston, Angela. *Birth and Reproduction.* Chicago: Heinemann Library, 1997.

ORGANIZATIONS

American Academy of Pediatrics
141 Northwest Point Boulevard
Elk Grove Village, IL 60007-1098
(847) 434-4000
www.aap.org

March of Dimes
Organization devoted to researching and educating about birth defetcts and threats to the health of newborn infants.
1275 Mamaroneck Avenue
White Plains, NY 10605
www.marchofdimes.com

INDEX